# TRAINING TO SUCCEED

# Football

# Edward Way

W

## FRANKLIN WATTS
LONDON • SYDNEY

First published in 2009 by
Franklin Watts
338 Euston Road
London NW1 3BH

Franklin Watts Australia
Level 17/207 Kent Street
Sydney NSW 2000

Words in **bold** are in the glossary on page 30.

**Series editor:** Sarah Peutrill
**Art director:** Jonathan Hair

Series designed and created for Franklin Watts by Storeybooks.
**Designer:** Rita Storey
**Editor:** Nicola Edwards
**Photography:** Tudor Photography, Banbury (unless otherwise stated)

**Picture credits**
© Bongarts/Getty Images p17; © 2008 Getty Images pp 24 and 26;
© 2008 AFP p27.
Emily supplied her own pictures on pp 5, 7, 8, 12, 14, 15, 18, 21, 22,
25, 27 and 28.
Every attempt has been made to clear copyright. Should there be any
inadvertent omission please apply to the publisher for rectification.

Thanks to Nottingham Forest Football club for the use of their
facilities. Also thanks to Emily, Karl, Nialle and Robbie for their
participation in the book.

A CIP catalogue record for this book is available from the British
Library.

Dewey classification: 796.334
ISBN: 978 0 7496 8429 7

Printed in China

Franklin Watts is a division of Hachette
Children's Books, an Hachette UK company.
www.hachette.co.uk

# Contents

Me and my sport                          4

Starting out                             6

The training ground                      8

Working with a coach                     10

Football skills                          12

Improving technique                      14

Working on tactics                       16

Sacrifices and setbacks                  18

Match preparation                        20

During the game                          22

Building experience                      24

My heroes                                26

Taking the next step                     28

Glossary                                 30

Find out more about football             31

Index                                    32

# Me and my sport

**Football is the world's most popular team sport. Played by tens of millions for fun, the top players are professional, paid large sums to play for top clubs in famous leagues in Europe and elsewhere.**

Many young, talented footballers dream of joining the ranks of professional players. Competition is fierce, though, and only the very best and most dedicated young footballers can hope to succeed. In this book, four footballers and their coach will share with you their experiences of training and performing on the pitch.

## Robbie Gibbons

Robbie is 16 and plays in central midfield. He moved from Dublin in the Republic of Ireland to play at the Nottingham Forest Academy and has played for the Ireland Under-16 team.

*I have three brothers who all still live at home in Dublin. My main interests other than football are **Gaelic football**, listening to music, playing computer games and going to the gym. Football has always been the main focus in my house. Whenever I played football it always made me feel happy. I never wanted to put the ball away because of the joy I got from having the ball at my feet.*

## Karl Darlow

Karl is a 17-year-old goalkeeper in his second year as an apprentice. He joined the Nottingham Forest Academy at 15, having previously been at Aston Villa. During the summer of 2008, Karl played for the Premier League Academy representative team at a tournament in Bosnia.

*I used to play football, rugby and cricket for my school and I also used to swim in my spare time. I always played football at school and my father had me playing all sports as a young lad, but you are always more interested in the sports you are good at, so football was a massive interest.*

## Nialle Rodney

Nialle is in the second year of his apprenticeship at Nottingham Forest Football Academy and plays as a **striker**. He joined the Academy at Under-13 level.

*I took up football because I enjoyed watching it when I was younger, and enjoyed playing it too. I also liked athletics at school and played for the school basketball and rugby teams. I also play tennis with the rest of the apprentices.*

## Life at the academy

Academies are special training centres and schemes set up by football clubs to help them develop young players. There are around 40 academies in Britain and many similar centres abroad. Karl, Nialle and Robbie are three of the 20 apprentices at the Nottingham Forest Football Academy all aged between 16 and 18 and all undertaking their two-year BTEC 'Apprenticeship in Sporting Excellence'. They train and compete as footballers, learn in the study centre classrooms for

## Emily Simpkins

Emily is 18 years old and works as a football coach going into schools in Derbyshire, England. She plays as a right back for Nottingham Forest Ladies having been signed from Leicester City Ladies in 2007.

*I used to do other sports, but not compete at a high standard like my football. I ran the 800m and 1500m for my school and did karate for two years. I always had a football at my feet when I was younger. I played football every break time and dinner time with all the boys in my class. I was the only girl all the time, but that didn't bother me. I support Derby County - Nottingham Forest's biggest rivals! I hate losing anything, whether the game is football or even cards!*

12 hours per week and play on Saturdays in the FA Premier Academy League. The apprentices live together in accommodation close to the club stadium, training ground and study centre.

*Emily with the Nottingham Forest Ladies team.*

*Robbie, Karl and Nialle at the academy training ground.*

# Starting out

Many footballers start out in their school team. If they perform well, they may join a local club or get a **trial** to play for a regional team. Every country and its football clubs have their own sets of football development schemes to train and improve talented young footballers. Sometimes, young players need a little bit of luck or good timing to be spotted by a coach or **scout** who can take them to a club or development centre offering a higher level of football coaching and competition.

*I trained at a local sports complex, and luckily we had a scout from a development centre working with us. I trained well and got the chance to go to the centre and then was given a six week trial at Aston Villa at the age of just seven.*

*I didn't start playing until I was eight years old. I was playing in the park by myself and was asked to join in with a team that were training on the next pitch; they were my first team, Pheasant Colts FC. I moved to a team called Priory Celtic at 10 and was with them until 13 when I was scouted by Forest, after scoring 54 goals in one season.*

Nialle moves forward with the ball under close control.

## Trials and contracts

*Many young players are assessed by football clubs at training and playing sessions known as trials. If successful, a young player may train and play with the club's youth teams. At 16 in the UK and many other countries, a footballer can be offered an apprenticeship agreement which may lead to a professional contract to play at a club.*

*When I made my debut for the Nottingham Forest **reserve team**, I was nervous and for the first 10–15 minutes you have to just try to do the basics right in order to get yourself involved in the game. After the first few minutes, I settled into the game and performed better.*

*I always remember being nervous, but as soon as that whistle went all the nerves disappeared and I just enjoyed the game. As a youngster I wasn't afraid of making mistakes, so even if I did something wrong, it wouldn't bother me, I would just get on with it and next time make sure I put it right.*

## Making the grade

Moving up a level to a better quality team is always a proud moment, but that first game for a new team can be daunting. How young footballers handle their first few appearances at a higher level may determine whether they will eventually be successful in the sport. The competition is fierce and many players are turned down along the way.

*I had received a few contract offers from clubs in England by the age of 16. I knew I was eligible to sign for one of them and move over full time to England, but really my decision to want to play football as my career came long before that. It was always my childhood dream.*

*Nialle shows good technique as he controls a falling ball with his chest.*

*It wasn't until I was at Priory at about age 12 that I realised I was good. Teams would put two **defenders** against me to try to stop me from scoring. At under 15/16 level, I realised this could be my job and that I wanted to keep playing at as high a level as possible.*

# The training ground

Working on the training ground is a vital part of a young footballer's week. Apprentice footballers at a major academy train almost every day. Training can be tough. There are some days when young players do not feel like rising to the challenge, but they know they must as training regularly and well is the only way to improve as footballers.

*We train every day except Wednesday (as we have education) and Sunday (day off). Monday and Tuesday we have double sessions, one in the morning and one in the afternoon. Each session is for about two hours each. Then on Thursday and Friday we just train once in the morning as it is closer to match day.*

*I think it's important that all players attend the training during the week to keep up fitness, to give all the players time to work on new things as a team and also to improve. The social side is also a great part of Nottingham Forest Ladies. We are a very close group of friends as well as team-mates.*

*The apprentices jog as part of their warm-up procedure before training.*

*Nialle sprints and weaves between cones as part of his speed and agility training.*

*The training has made me a lot fitter, and it has changed my lifestyle, because I need to make sure that I have enough energy for training. I am a lot stronger and quicker, which is needed for the modern game, and have improved my game understanding, for example the tactics of defending from the front.*

**A typical day at the Nottingham Forest Football Academy**
Report in: 8.00am
Gym work: 8.15am–9.00am
Education at the Study Centre:
9.00–10.00am
Training: 10.30am–12 noon
Lunch: 12 noon–1pm
Training: 1.30pm–3pm

## Taking care

Players are expected to look after the kit they use, from their boots and shinpads to the training clothing they wear in different weather conditions.

Top coaches structure the training carefully, making sure that players have warmed up and stretched their muscles beforehand to prevent injuries.

*The kit I use includes boots, which I clean every day for training and match days, and goalkeeper gloves, which I tend to wash once a week or whenever I feel the need to. In my training bag I keep shin pads, so they are never forgotten, and a water bottle which keeps me hydrated throughout training sessions.*

# Working with a coach

Coaches are crucial to the development of successful young footballers. They are in charge of all the players' training sessions, choosing what skills and techniques are covered in each one. They also oversee the players' physical fitness and development and can offer mental and emotional support for young footballers.

## Meet the coach: Chris Fairclough

Chris Fairclough played over 130 first team games as a central defender for Nottingham Forest, during which period he also played seven times for the England Under-21 team. He moved to Spurs in 1987 and then on to Leeds United for whom he played 240 games and won 1990 Player of the Year. He moved to Bolton Wanderers in 1995.

Chris is now Under-18 coach at Nottingham Forest Football Academy. He is a highly successful coach who holds the high level UEFA A Licence coaching qualification.

His motto to his players in training is, "Enjoy working hard!"

*Coach Chris Fairclough takes the apprentices through a passing move. Coaches who are experienced ex-professional footballers frequently demonstrate moves to players.*

*I can't say a bad word about our coach, he is top class. He has taken me at Under-16 and Under-18 levels and has improved me as a player and person; he is a very good role model. I always know what he wants and what his expectations are.*

*Nialle helps support Robbie as he lifts weights in the gym. The players are working on their strength and building their core stability.*

### Core stability
*Your core is your body's torso or trunk which consists of more than 30 separate muscles across your back, stomach and hips. Strengthening these muscles gives a footballer a more stable base to run and stretch against, increasing fitness and potential speed.*

*Not only do we do actual football training, but we now do other types of training, such as weight training, flexibility sessions and* **core stabilisation training***, which are all key in becoming a modern day footballer. All this training helps you in becoming a better athlete, making you faster and stronger, which is so important nowadays.*

**Coach's notes: attributes**
*Talent alone will rarely get someone to the top of their chosen sport. You need mental attributes such as dedication, mental strength and intelligence and physical attributes such as speed, agility and strength. All these help to make a modern footballer.*

## All-round improvement
Out on the training ground, footballers work on their skills (see pages 12–15), speed, their understanding of the game (see pages 16–17 – tactics) and **stamina** – the ability to exercise hard for long periods of time. Their coach also oversees other areas of training, often handing over his players to specialists in areas such as diet and nutrition, sports psychology and gym work to build strength and flexibility – increasing the range of movement in the players' bodies.

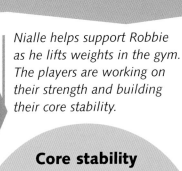

*We do weight training for strength in the club gym with the academy fitness trainer, and flexibility sessions with the academy* **physiotherapist***. We also have a* **sports psychologist** *to improve our mental approach.*

# Football skills

As well as being physically fit, fast and strong, a footballer needs to have excellent skills and understanding of the game. Techniques are worked on and improved on the training ground. Footballers continue to work on their key skills and techniques throughout their careers.

## Controlling the ball

The most fundamental football skills are controlling the ball and passing it to a team-mate. Players apart from the goalkeeper can control the ball with any part of the body except the hands and arms, depending on the height and angle at which it arrives. With the first touch of the ball a footballer aims to get it under control so that he or she can pass, shoot or run with the ball without delay. An improved first touch only comes with hundreds of hours of practice and training.

*As a goalkeeper there are many different areas to work on: handling, low dives, high dives, reaction saves, **crossing**, kicking and communication. The training is normally built up throughout the session with greater repetition and more sets of moves in order to make the training harder. It also helps you to concentrate when you are tired in a match.*

Karl uses the inside of his boot to control and bring down the ball. Goalkeepers practise their ball control and kicking skills for match situations.

*I try and practise as much as possible. My best friend at the minute is the brick wall in my back garden, I spend so much time there. By hitting the ball at the wall hard, it gives me a chance to improve my first touch. If I want to make it tougher for myself, I just hit it harder against the wall or stand closer.*

## Passing and heading

Players work hard on their passing so that they can pass quickly and accurately and send the ball to the receiver in ways that are easy to control. Slick, accurate passing can unlock an opposing team's defence and players learn to make different length and strength passes with both feet. Goalkeepers often have to clear the ball or pass it, so also work on improving their kicking with both feet. Players work on a range of different headers from powerful defensive headers, which clear the ball a long distance upfield, to glancing headers which send the ball off at an angle.

*Robbie hits away a strong header. He keeps his eyes following the ball and aims to regain his balance as quickly as possible to get back in the game.*

*For attacking headers, we practise a lot trying to head at goal from crosses (high passes from wide on the pitch made into the opposing team's **penalty area**). This helps you get your headers on target to try and score goals. For defensive headers, we tend to work in twos, and just throw the ball into the air for our partner to get a big header on it.*

*I get a defender to play long balls and short fast passes into me to practise my control with all areas of the body – your decision-making when controlling the ball is important.*

*Nialle makes a pass during training with his body weight over the ball to keep it skimming across the grass.*

13

# Improving technique

Goals win football games. So it is not surprising that many of the skills worked on at the training ground are to do with attacking and scoring goals and defending to prevent goals being scored.

*My favourite shot is the **half volley**. When you connect with it perfectly, it looks quality and can create so much power.*

## Shooting practice

It is not just a team's strikers that practise their shooting. Any of the outfield players (the ten players in a team besides the goalkeeper) may get the chance to shoot during a game so all take part in shooting drills. Shooting practice is designed to help hone a footballer's power, accuracy and decision-making when shooting.

**Coach notes: shooting**
When shooting, make sure you keep the ball on target and try to get your body over the ball to stop your shots sailing high. Always stay alert and follow up your shot in case the ball rebounds out. You may get a second chance!

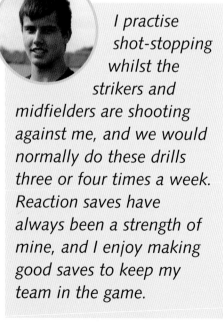

*I practise shot-stopping whilst the strikers and midfielders are shooting against me, and we would normally do these drills three or four times a week. Reaction saves have always been a strength of mine, and I enjoy making good saves to keep my team in the game.*

Nialle hits a strong shot, aiming for the bottom left corner of the goal.

A player often only gets a fraction of a second to take a shot, so many drills emphasise taking quick reaction shots or running onto a pass from another player and taking a shot on the move. Shooting drills also give goalkeepers lots of valuable shot-stopping practice.

## Drilling defending skills

Defenders need to show individual skill and discipline as part of a team. When a team loses the ball, all the members of the team have tasks to perform in defence. Defence is more than just tackling and challenging for the ball. Players also have to learn to **jockey** opponents with the ball, slowing them down and trying to guide them away from danger. This gives the defender's team-mates the time to regroup and get into good defensive positions.

*Emily shields the ball from a strong challenge.*

*Strikers are the first defenders in the team so I do work on defending. It's important to understand the opposition's tactics so that you can close them down and show the right way for the rest of the team.*

*We do 1 v 1 and 2 v 2 drills in defending because it's important that you are able to defend correctly and jockey your opponent. The key factors when jockeying are to make sure you are down low, light on your feet, patient and to make sure you don't get caught by surprise by your opponent performing a trick or a **dummy**.*

*Karl jumps and stretches to catch a cross before it falls and can be reached by an opponent.*

# Working on tactics

Football is a highly tactical game, as one team attempts to play in ways which will outwit the opposition. A team's manager or coach decides on a team's tactics, selects the players who start and determines how they will play.

*We do practise different formations because Chris knows that throughout the season, against different opposition teams, we will have to play in different ways.*

## Formations

A team's **formation** is how it lines up in terms of defenders, midfielders and strikers. It is shown in numbers, so for example 4-1-3-2 means that a team is playing with four defenders, one defensive midfielder, three midfielders and two strikers. Teams may play using one formation most of the time, but are likely to train using a variety of formations.

*Robbie looks for a free team-mate as he takes a throw-in.*

*Last season we changed from 4-4-2 to 4-3-3 with a defensive midfield player against Everton, and it changed the game. It gave us more stability and allowed more attacks down the middle.*

## Team tactics

A team's formation is just the beginning of the tactics a team can employ. A coach may recommend that a team plays a short 'pass and move' game with lots of passes and the players keeping control and **possession** of the ball. Other coaches may favour a more direct game where the ball is passed long and early to the strikers up front. Tactics and formations can be changed during the game as well, so players need to listen to communications and signals from their coach and team-mates.

## Set pieces

Set pieces are ways in which a football match is re-started after a stoppage due to a **foul** or the ball going out of play. Two key **set pieces**, corners and free kicks, can offer good opportunities to score. Even throw-ins from the sideline can turn into dangerous attacking moves when rehearsed in training and executed well. Teams practise set-piece moves that aim to surprise the opposition, and also practise defending typical set pieces such as corners.

*We mainly go through tactics on a Monday morning in our debrief or on Friday morning on the training ground. On the Saturday morning, Chris will stick up different posters on the wall of the dressing room to show who goes where for defensive and attacking set pieces.*

*We have set positions when defending a corner kick and then pick up opponents the best we can within those ranges. From free kicks it varies because of positioning and the number of players in the* **wall***.*

*Croatia have formed a three-man wall to cut down the angles for Switzerland's Yakin as he takes a free kick.*

# Sacrifices and setbacks

Young footballers have to make many sacrifices during their career. They have to watch what they eat and drink, have less leisure time than other teenagers and may have to live close to their football club and away from their family and friends. Most, though, think all the sacrifice and effort is worth it.

*We have a very busy week, and seem to fit it all in, and we get Sundays off. I have no regrets.*

## Dealing with setbacks

Footballers are likely to have to overcome setbacks in their career. These can range from a serious injury to struggling to improve their game or even losing their place in a team. Footballers need to follow advice from their coach and physio when trying to recover their form or from an injury. Robbie suffered a torn ankle ligament on the day he moved to the Academy and signed his contract. He was out for over three months – a distressing time for him.

*I don't go out as much as I would like to. All I do is work, train, play and in any spare time I like to relax and go to the gym. No regrets! Football comes first.*

*It's the worst feeling ever not being able to play and watching all your team-mates train every day whilst you're in the physio room on your own doing nothing. But the only thing you can do is keep thinking positive and work your very hardest to get back to fitness.*

*Karl takes a drink of water during training to keep up his fluid levels.*

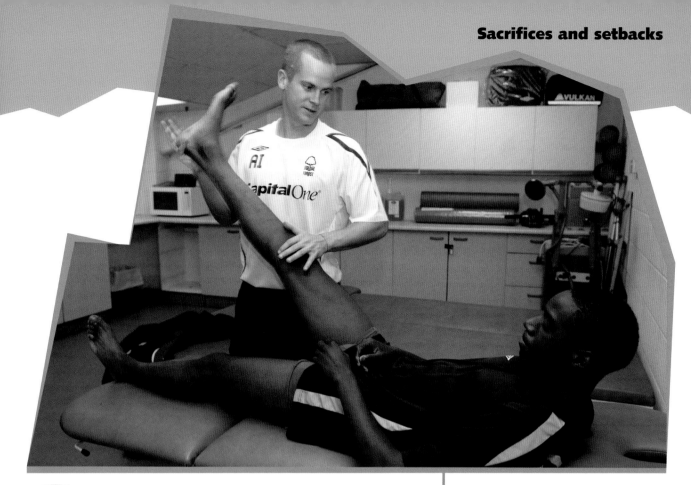

*A player has a **hamstring** injury assessed by the club physiotherapist.*

*I live away from my family and education is fitted in on a Wednesday and Thursday afternoon, but I also do some work in my own time. I'm never out late at a weekend. I eat a lot of fruit and take on a lot of water whilst training. I live in digs (supervised accommodation) so they control what I eat, really.*

### Coach's notes: eat well

Young, non-professional footballers will be fine with a healthy, well-balanced diet, trying to incorporate at least five pieces of fruit and vegetables daily. Loading meals with carbohydrates such as pasta, rice or potatoes is a good idea to help boost your energy stores before a match.

## Football and food

Football is a high-energy, high-intensity sport and players need to eat very carefully and very healthily to get the maximum benefit out of their meals. Lean meats, fish, fresh vegetables and fruits are on the menu. Fast foods full of fat and sugar are out, although energy drinks and snack bars are a good source of energy during a long training day.

# Match preparation

A week's training is designed to improve a footballer's overall abilities, but is also tailored to producing a good performance in the next big match. Each player prepares mentally and physically with great care in the period before a match.

*We arrive at the ground one hour before kick-off. We do a team warm-up of jogging, sprints, stretches and ball work and then I do my own sprints before kick-off.*

*Our preparation for the match on Saturday starts on the Sunday before. Everything you do has to be totally professional throughout the whole week for the best possible performance on Saturday. You have to work hard in every training session and be disciplined in what you eat and the times you go to bed.*

## At the ground

The final preparation begins when players arrive at the ground. They change into their kit, go out onto the pitch and perform a warm-up with some sprinting and agility exercises. They also perform a series of stretches to their muscles which prepares them for the hard work ahead and helps prevent pulled muscles and other injuries.

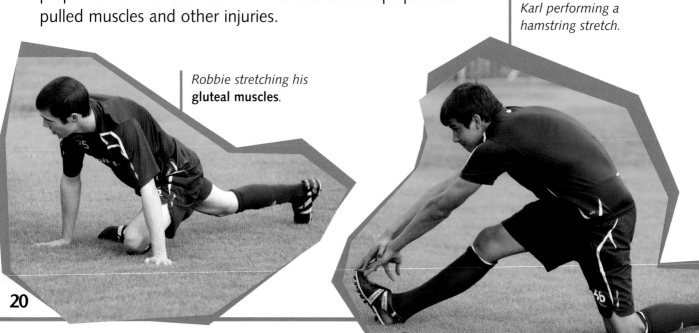

*Robbie stretching his* **gluteal muscles**.

*Karl performing a hamstring stretch.*

## Preparation in the changing room

Back in the changing room for the last few minutes before the match, the players listen carefully to their coach's team talk and try to stay positive and focused about the game ahead. Nerves are common, whilst some footballers are superstitious and always prepare in the same way or wear the same 'lucky' items of clothing.

### Coach's notes: pre-season

Pre-season sees the players report back in July. We get players physically prepared and as 'match ready' as possible for the start of the coming season in August. Pre-season consists of running, football training, weight training, practice matches and team-building days.

*Nialle and Karl talk tactics while they get ready to play.*

*Myself and any other goalkeepers go out for half an hour, do some jogs and stretching, basic handling, pick ups from the floor, passing, low saves right and left, half volleys, strikes off the deck, crosses and finally kicking.*

*I use my iPod and listen to my favourite songs to motivate me. I use sounds that remind me of certain things, for example, replaying the song that was played before the game that got my team promoted last season into the national Women's Premier League.*

# During the game

Karl, Robbie and Nialle play in the Academy Premier League whilst Emily plays in the Women's Premier League. All four come up against highly talented opponents as they play against the other Academy teams such as Manchester United, Everton and, in Emily's case, Arsenal Ladies.

## Under pressure

Players may find themselves under severe pressure in many matches as their team goes one or more goals down. Keeping confidence in themselves and their team-mates is crucial in these situations as a team tries to regroup and get back into the game. Players should support rather than snipe at a team-mate who has made a bad mistake or who is struggling.

*It's a wonderful feeling when you are running out before a game, and I think you are just hoping that you can perform well and help your team get the three points.*

*Just before kick-off, the **adrenalin** is flowing and I just want to get myself involved in the game and do something well early on.*

*We're a team – we help and support each other all over the pitch. As players we never feel on our own. Playing at the highest level, there is always lots of pressure whatever team we play, so we just have to relax when we are on the ball and play as well as we know we can. And if one player is having a poor game, we have to help her through it.*

*Emily shouts instructions to a team-mate during a training game. Players must communicate with each other for their team to perform at its best.*

## Half-time

The 15-minute half-time period is a time for players to catch their breath, rest and take onboard a little water, juice or sports drink. They also listen to any instructions or team talk given by the coach. Coaches may make small or large changes to the team's tactics at half-time so players have to concentrate hard and adjust the way in which they play during the second half.

*Team talks at half-time can vary. The coach will ask how we are doing and then give his key points and expectations for the second half.*

*If you are up against a team that keeps the ball really well and you are chasing it for long periods, it is really important that you are able to keep it when you win it back. I think if you are up against a really good player you just have to be intelligent about how you defend against him and stay patient, not diving in and letting him beat you easily.*

*Small-sided football games in training encourage constant involvement by all the players taking part. This helps build players' skills and confidence for when they're involved in a big game.*

# Building experience

Footballers reflect on how a game went and how they performed. Learning from game experiences is a crucial part of a young footballer's development.

## Game debriefing

Some teams discuss how the game went straight after a match. However, many teams and coaches prefer to analyse performances when players aren't so tired. A good coach will run through key points in a match, often using video clips to highlight good and poor aspects of play by the team and individuals.

*Every Monday morning after our match on the Saturday, we will sit down and have a debrief and watch the highlights from the weekend as we have a video analyst who records every game. In this meeting, we will go through what we did well so we can repeat it in the next match, and what we didn't do so well, so hopefully we can improve on it for the next game.*

*When substituted, you feel disappointment that you have to leave the game. The fact that you can no longer have an impact on the game is hard to take. But you have to deal with the decision and try to set your aim not to get substituted next match.*

*Being substituted is hard for any player to take but it is all part of football's tactical process.*

## Not going as planned

Matches often don't go quite as planned for a team or an individual. Sometimes, young players will have a poor game or come up against a better player or team than themselves. They may get substituted or involved in a clash which results in them being sent off. They may feel down after their side is defeated heavily. But young players, guided by their coach and team-mates, need to learn from these hurtful experiences to become stronger characters and better footballers.

*I have been sent off once when I was playing for Leicester City Ladies, aged 15. It was for a handball on the goal line to prevent the opposition scoring. I felt so small having to walk back to the changing rooms. It felt like everybody was watching me.*

### Coach's notes: talent

Always remember the talent and qualities that got you to where you are today!

Promise yourself that you will build on that talent, and always reflect on each game to assess your performance, whether it was poor, average or excellent.

*A coach will talk through a match or individual performances with the players and can also demonstrate mistakes or improvements in training.*

# My heroes

Football is a sport that turns players into heroes for the fans of every club and national team. A child's first hero as a footballer can have a big effect on the way he or she learns to play football.

*My heroes today are Pelé because he was unique as a player and an unbelievable footballer. I also admire Emmanuel Adebayor – I aspire to be like him.*

*My first football hero was Ronaldo (the Brazilian striker). I used to watch him play for Inter Milan and Barcelona when I was a kid, and he used to have so much skill, pace and power and he was clinical in front of the goal.*

*Striker Emmanuel Adebayor in action for Arsenal. He also plays for his country – Togo.*

*My hero is David James. He's a great kicker of the ball, extremely athletic, makes terrific saves and communicates with his team-mates well. He's also shown great character to come back from taunts to now being first choice for England.*

*Paul Scholes vies with Zenit St Petersburg's Konstantin Zyryanov during their European Super Cup football match in 2008.*

*My heroes now are Paul Scholes and Roy Keane. I admire Paul Scholes because he is such a wonderful professional and you never hear anything bad about him. To be able to play as consistently as he has for as long as he has at the very top level is just incredible. Roy Keane's determination and attitude to win games was unbelievable. I think I try to copy Scholes with his passing ability and movement and intelligence to get on the ball, and with Keane, I try to copy his attitude of always working hard.*

## Learning from heroes

Heroes don't have to disappear as you grow older. Many professional footballers have players that they admire for their attitude, skills or performances. Watching their heroes play can give an aspiring professional footballer tips on techniques or tactics as well as the inspiration to improve and reach the heights their heroes have reached.

*My hero is my dad. He is very much my best friend but also my worst enemy! My dad and granddad both played for a local club which was in the Central Midlands League.*

# Taking the next step

Football is an intensely competitive sport. Young footballers cannot sit back and relax for fear of being overtaken by others. Previous success is no guarantee of keeping their place in a team, getting a professional contract at a football club or moving up a level.

Coaches urge players to keep working hard on their fitness and skills. Short term and longer term targets are set. Players aim to improve certain parts of their game, such as their passing with their weaker foot, and their fitness.

*Emily and her team-mate Natalie with the Northern Premier League Cup.*

*My aim is to be a permanent fixture within the reserve team, as this will help recognition with the first team manager, and other clubs. In the longer term, I hope to be playing regularly for a Championship club at least.*

*I want to try and improve on everything I do on my weaker foot, my shooting, my passing and my turning. It is so important to be good on both sides as a central midfielder if you want to play at the highest level.*

*I always try and practise the latest trick that has been done in the Premiership. I want to work on being able to beat a player, then the next player and so on. I want to be the best player on the pitch every game I play in. In five years' time I hope to be playing for England, and be the best and most well known female footballer.*

## Career targets

Players set themselves goals or targets for their career and where they would like to be in the seasons ahead. For many players at a professional club academy, the first goal is to get into the academy side, to shine and progress into the adult reserve team. The hope is then that their performances will be good enough to win them appearances for the first team.

If they succeed, there will be many further challenges ahead, from holding down a place in a club's first team, to being a positive role model for others and dealing with the media and public attention that can come with being a young football star.

*To be a top role model in football, you have to have a wonderful attitude on and off the pitch. You have to show professionalism at all times, you have to show character, have great discipline, be honest, show commitment in everything you do and be motivated to be the best you can be. I feel I would be a good role model because I have a good attitude on and off the pitch and I always try to give one hundred per cent in everything I do.*

*My career targets are to earn a pro contract at the end of this season and in five years, to be playing for a big club and playing international football.*

*Robbie, Karl and Nialle reflect on a tiring but enjoyable training session. All three hope to have a long and successful career in professional football.*

# Glossary

**adrenalin** A hormone that is released into the body at times of stress or excitement. It can help an athlete by boosting the supply of oxygen and glucose to the brain and muscles.

**core stabilisation training** Strengthening core muscles in the trunk of the body to help prevent injuries.

**crossing** Passing and sending the ball from the edge of the pitch into the centre of the field.

**defenders** Players whose main responsibility is preventing goals being scored by the opposition.

**dummy** Using fake moves of the body to pretend to do one thing but instead, do another.

**formation** The way a team lines up in terms of defenders, midfielders and forwards.

**foul** A breaking of one of the laws of football, often some sort of outlawed challenge on an opposition player.

**Gaelic football** A type of football from and mainly played in Ireland featuring 15 players a side.

**gluteal muscles** The muscles in the buttocks region.

**half volley** To kick the ball just as it hits the ground.

**hamstring** The large muscle located at the back of the thigh.

**jockey** To use techniques to delay an opponent with the ball.

**penalty area** A rectangular area 13m wide and 16.5m deep in front of each goal.

**physiotherapist** Also known as a physio, a trained specialist who deals with injuries using massage, exercises and other physical treatments.

**possession** When one team has control of the football.

**pre-season** A period before the start of the regular competitive season where players assemble and train hard to work on fitness and their skills.

**reserve team** A team below the level of a club's first team, often with younger and less-experienced players.

**scout** A knowledgeable person, often a coach or ex-coach, who watches matches to spot young football talent.

**set pieces** Ways of restarting a game such as a throw-in, corner and free kick. Many set pieces offer a good opportunity for one team to attack and score.

**sports psychologist** A psychologist who specialises in working with sportspeople to improve their performance.

**stamina** The ability to maintain physical effort over a long period of time.

**striker** Attack-minded player whose main job is to set up and score goals.

**trial** A match or session designed to help a coach pick players for a club or team.

**wall** A line of defenders standing together to protect their goal against a free kick by the opposing team.

# Find out more about football

## Books

**Soccer Coaching The Professional Way – Malcolm Cook (A&C Black, 2006)**
An in-depth guide by an ex-professional coach on how coaches scout, train and motivate their players.

**Ajax Training Sessions – J. Smink (Reedswain Incorporated, 2004)**
An unusual and interesting look into the drills and training techniques used at the famous Dutch football club, Ajax FC.

**Know Your Sport: Football – Clive Gifford (Franklin Watts, 2006)**
An introductory guide to the essential skills and tactics needed to play effective football.

**The Soccer Goalkeeping Handbook: The Essential Guide for Players and Coaches – Alex Welsh (A&C Black, 2004)**
An excellent training manual for goalkeepers with useful tips, techniques and training drills.

**Soccer Training For Women and Girls – Klaus Bischops and Heinz-Willi Gerards (Meyer & Meyer Sports Books, 2003)**
A useful guide for budding female footballers.

## DVDs and websites

**Soccer Superskills with Jay Jay Okocha (Sony Pictures, 2004)**
African soccer legend Okocha, together with talented youngsters from Brazilian soccer schools, take the viewer through many of the skills needed to play good football.

**www.nflfc.co.uk**
The website of Nottingham Forest Ladies football club where Emily plays.

**www.nottinghamforest.premiumtv.co.uk/page/AcademyNews**
The homepages of the Academy where Karl, Robbie and Nialle all play.

**www.insidesoccer.com**
A very useful football video site with plenty of video clips of training drills, moves and tactics used in football.

**www.thefa.com/GrassrootsNew**
This section of the Football Association's website features pages on nutrition and pre-season training, as well as a database to help you find a local football club.

**www.fgmag.com**
Homepage of the women's football magazine, *Fair Game*, with fixtures, results and news from women's clubs and academies.

**www.grassrootscoaching.com/links**
An excellent collection of links to other websites organised into groups including football coaching, women's football, soccer in Australia and USA junior soccer.

**www.givemefootball.com**
The website of the Professional Footballers Association (PFA) is packed with features on the top players of the past and present, the latest football news and player and manager interviews.

**www.jbgoalkeeping.com/links.html**
A very useful website for goalkeepers with a large collection of drills, exercises and tips for goalkeeping.

**www.fifa.com/en/index.html**
The official website for FIFA, the organization that runs world football.

# Index

academies   5, 8, 29
Adebayor, Emmanuel   26
apprenticeships   5, 6

ball control   12

career targets   29
coaches   10–11, 16, 21, 23
contracts   6
core stability training   11, 30
corners   17
crosses   13, 30

defenders   7, 15, 30
diet   19
dummy   14, 30

experience   24–5

Fairclough, Chris   10, 17
flexibility   11
football development
    schemes   6
formations   16, 30
fouls   25, 30
free kicks   17

Gaelic football   4, 30
game debriefing   24–5
games   22–3
goalkeepers   12, 13, 15, 21

half-time   23
half volley   13, 30
heading   13
heroes   26–7

James, David   26
jockey   15, 30

Keane, Roy   27
kicking skills   12, 13
kit   9

managers   16
match preparation   20–1
mental attributes   11
muscles   11, 20

Nottingham Forest Football
    Academy   5, 9

outfield players   14

pass and move   16
passing   10, 12, 13
Pelé   26
penalty area   30
physical attributes   11
physiotherapists   11, 19, 30
possession   16, 30
pre-season   21, 30
pressure   22

reserve team   7, 30
role models   29
Ronaldo   26

sacrifices   18
Scholes, Paul   27
scouts   6, 30
set pieces   17, 30
setbacks   18–19
shooting   14–15

shot-stopping   14, 15
skills   12–13, 14–15
speed and agility   9, 11
sports psychologists   11, 30
stamina   11, 30
strength   11
stretches   20
strikers   5, 15, 26, 30
substitutions   24, 25

tactics   10, 16–17, 21, 23
talent   6, 25
targets   28–9
teamwork   15, 22
technique   7, 12, 14–15
throw-ins   16, 17
training   8–9, 10–11
trials   6, 30

wall   17, 30
warming up   8, 9, 20
water   18, 19, 23
weight-training   11

Zyryanov, Konstantin   27